G000292702

Springs of Love

Blake

Byron

Goethe

Rilke

Shakespeare

Stendhal

Search Press Ltd, England
Kampmann & Company Inc, New York

Copyright by Leobuchhandlung, CH-St. Gallen

Love seeketh
not itself to
        please
Nor for itself hath
    any care,
But for
another
  gives its ease
    And builds
    a heaven in
    hell's despair.

WILLIAM BLAKE

ALL WHO JOY
WOULD
WIN
MUST SHARE
IT –
HAPPINESS
WAS BORN
A TWIN

BYRON

To be able to find joy in another's joy :
that is the secret of happiness. GEORGES BERNANOS

Pains of
love
be sweeter
far
Than all other
pleasures
are.

JOHN DRYDEN

The world
is so empty if
one thinks only of mountains,
rivers and cities; but to know
someone here and there who
thinks and feels with us, and
who, though distant, is close
to us in spirit, this makes the
earth for us an
inhabited garden.

JOHANN WOLFGANG GOETHE

What charms
are there
in the harmony
of minds,
and in a friendship
founded
on mutual
esteem and
gratitude.

DAVID HUME

It is not the perfect, but the imperfect,
who have need of love.

OSCAR WILDE

NEVER CEASE LOVING A
PERSON, AND NEVER GIVE
UP HOPE FOR HIM,
FOR EVEN THE PRODIGAL
SON WHO HAD FALLEN
        MOST LOW,
COULD STILL BE SAVED;
THE BITTEREST ENEMY
AND ALSO HE WHO WAS
YOUR FRIEND COULD
AGAIN BE YOUR FRIEND;
        LOVE
THAT HAS GROWN COLD
CAN KINDLE AGAIN.

        SÖREN KIERKEGAARD

Time and again man
stands before the abyss
    of eternal solitude.

Not even love and friendship
can halt the inevitable
cycle of growth and decay,
joy and sorrow,
    longing and fulfilment.

The inconstancy of Me and
You requires of us each day
    indulgence and
sacrifice, and that we strive
    after mutual
    Affection
    and Love.

NICO

There is but one
       salvation for
the tired soul :
       love for another
person.

For what is love, but ~
the lover makes
       the soul of his
beloved his sphere
       and they are
one in spirit.

JOSÉ ORTEGA Y GASSET

Love sought is good, but given
unsought is better.

SHAKESPEARE

Let those
love now
who never
loved before.
Let those
who always
loved
now love
the more.

THOMAS PARNELL

Love
consists in this:
that two
    solitudes
protect and
    touch and
greet each
    other.

RAINER MARIA RILKE

LOVE !
The most divine
gift man possesses,
when it
is devotion of
self;
The most foolish
and disappointing,
when it is nothing
but the pursuit
of happiness.

ROMAIN ROLLAND

Friendship is the wine of life.

EDWARD YOUNG

Even if you had failings,
I should be forbearing.
It is not love when one
simply draws a beautiful
picture in one's soul and
endows it with every
perfection, rather this is
love: to love people as we
find them, and if they have
weaknesses, to accept them
with a heart filled with

Love.

CHARLOTTE TO SCHILLER

LOVE
IS A BURDEN,
WHICH TWO HEARTS,
WHEN
EQUALLY THEY
BEAR
THEIR PARTS,
WITH PLEASURE
CARRY:
BUT NO ONE, ALAS!
CAN BEAR
IT ALONE.

CHARLES SEDLEY

Love is a well from
which we can
drink
only as much as we
have put in,
and the stars that
shine from
it are only our eyes
looking in.

STENDHAL

Real love begins where nothing is
expected in return.

ANTOINE DE SAINT-EXUPERY

'TIS SWEET
TO FEEL BY
WHAT FINE
SPUN THREADS
OUR AFFECTIONS
ARE DRAWN
TOGETHER.

LAURENCE STERNE

Come what may
As long as you live,
          it is day.
And if I in the world
          must roam,
Wherever you are,
          that is home.
When your loving
          voice I hear
The future's shadows
          disappear.

THEODOR STORM

Precious little gifts of lasting value.

In the same series:

SPRINGS OF COMFORT
SPRINGS OF FRIENDSHIP
SPRINGS OF HAPPINESS
SPRINGS OF HOPE
SPRINGS OF INDIAN WISDOM
SPRINGS OF JAPANESE WISDOM
SPRINGS OF MUSIC
SPRINGS OF ORIENTAL WISDOM
SPRINGS OF PERSIAN WISDOM
SPRINGS OF JOY
SPRINGS OF JEWISH WISDOM
AFFECTION, FRIENDSHIP AND LOVE
IN PRAISE OF BEAUTY

Texts chosen by E. Hettinger
Translated by Dr. Peter M. Daly
Designer J. Tannheimer

Distribution:
UK: Search Press Ltd., England
USA: Kampmann & Company Inc., New York

Copyright 1986 by Leobuchhandlung, CH-St.Gallen
Modèle déposé, BIRPI
Printed in Switzerland

.